Tribute to a Common Man

C. STEVEN ROAF

iUniverse, Inc.
Bloomington

Tribute to a Common Man

iUniverse books may be ordered through booksellers or by contacting:

*iUniverse
1663 Liberty Drive
Bloomington, IN 47403
www.iuniverse.com
1-800-Authors (1-800-288-4677)*

ISBN: 978-1-4502-9402-7 (sc)
ISBN: 978-1-4502-9401-0 (ebook)

Printed in the United States of America

iUniverse rev. date: 3/30/2011

ACKNOWLEDGMENT

I wish to thank my brother and friend Warren for believing in me always. I also wish to acknowledge my ancestors, known and unknown, as a tribute to their legacy.

CONTENTS

INTRODUCTION

The idea for this book came to me during a period of early morning hours when I couldn't sleep. My thoughts had drifted to my grandfather and how he influenced me as a mentor, a second father, a friend, a companion, a teacher, a guidance counselor, a hero, and a role model. I do not think he was fully aware of all this while alive, and though he has been gone from this Earth some twenty-five years, his lessons still echo in my thoughts and memory. He could be gruff or comical. He had, at times, the anger of a raging bull and at other times an impish smile and twinkle in his eye that gave away his mischievous intentions.

He was born into a broken home and lived a somewhat obscure life, and the question comes to mind, "What is the purpose of the life of such a common man?" To answer the question, I delve into the memories and stories as I knew them and leave you to answer the all-important question, "What is the purpose of your life?" Further, can the traditional values we once were taught serve us today in a society full of distractions and self-centered affluence? I will leave those answers for you to decide as well.

My quest started some time ago when I went in search of a long-held family secret. I was in search of my roots and wanted to shed some light on my own ancestry, which my surname did not represent. I found the answer to my question, at least partly, and the big skeleton in the closet. It started with an unwed mother in Victorian-era New England and her illegitimate son. The boy of humble beginnings led a life of hard work and grew to be a man, not famous or wealthy, but one who inspired, enjoyed life, and left a legacy that should not be forgotten. Not openly affectionate but with a heart of gold, he was known to people as a man of his word. In that, he had honor and respect. To him I dedicate this book.

CHAPTER I
THE IRISH BULL

I always picture my grandfather sitting in our kitchen with his blue farm overalls, armless T-shirt, and brown, almost always muddy shoes. He often "smelled of the barn," which drove my mother absolutely crazy. It wasn't a condition of hygiene so much as a condition of life where he had accumulated the musty smells of hay, good farm dirt, and wood-burning stove and a lifetime of hard toil. It was almost a cologne to me, a manly smell that filled my nostrils and that no amount of soap would ever wash away.

Grampa at Mom's table in overalls.

It was usually in the evening hours when Gramps would come in for a visit. With the cow milked and the wood brought in, he would have finished a long day in the garden, ending with his final chores in the barn. Ma would tell him in very clear terms to wipe his feet and would not allow him to sit anywhere but the kitchen, so that he wouldn't "track through the house." He only wanted to visit and talk. But no matter the subject of the conversation, it always seemed to end up with my father saying to Grampa, "Yeah, yeah, you know everything," when my grandfather would merely be offering his advice on a particular matter. Gramps loved to just sit and visit and talk and see his grandchildren. But there was always that bit of tension in the air, and it took me quite a few years to analyze it and figure it out.

My grandparents lived in the other half of the house, where the common walls of the duplex allowed us to hear when an argument was taking place in the other side. There weren't too many secrets that could be kept from one side of the family or the other. If we kids were upstairs in our bedrooms, we could hear conversations as if we were in the same room. Part of this was due to the heating grates cut in the floor of the upstairs and ceiling of the downstairs that allowed the heat from downstairs to heat the bedrooms upstairs. My father hated being told what to do, even by his own father, and when the conversation became heated, my mother would always say that the stubbornness both displayed was because of the "Irish bull" in them both. "You're just like your father," she would tell my dad. He hated hearing her say that, but upon reflection, I would have to say it was true.

We lived in what is called a duplex in New England, a century-old mill house built when the textile industry was at its peak in early twentieth-century New England, when villages were built around the mills where the factory workers spent their lives. The houses eventually sold to even non-mill workers. Very small in comparison to today's houses, "upstairs" had two fairly normal-for-the-time bedrooms and a much smaller room no bigger than what one today would consider a walk-in closet. There were no built-in closets because the old-style homes were still European, in that people had freestanding wardrobes for storage space. Each room had a slanted ceiling caused by the sloping peak of the roof. My parents had one bedroom, my brother and I shared the other larger room, and my sister had the much smaller room to herself. There was one small bathroom with a tub (no shower) and a sink, which we all shared. On the first floor was a kitchen; a small den, as we referred to it; and the formal parlor where as young kids we were not allowed to sit without adults. Needless to say, there was not much room for a family of five to live in. The 1950s decor of our side of the house, with its linoleum floors and chrome kitchen table, highlighted the decades of difference between the two sides.

The old white, clapboard-sided house was built circa 1890 with a dirt cellar that used to store coal for heating in the old days. We stored potatoes through the winter along with canned vegetables from the garden. I often had to go to the cellar, and I remember the distinct damp, earthy smell mixed with the fumes from the fifty-gallon drums of kerosene that we used to heat our side of the house. Descending the narrow, steep, rickety wooden stairs, I had to duck my head so as to not catch a beam across the brow, and I quite often took a spiderweb in the face instead. By squeezing through the boards that separated the two halves of the cellar, I could get into my grandparents' side of the house. They burned wood, not heating oil, for heat, but there was residual coal lying on the floor that was of great curiosity to me. I tried to imagine what it would have been like to be Superman and squeeze the lumps of coal until they turned to diamonds in my hands.

On the other side of the house, the mirror image of our side, was where my grandparents lived with my aunt and later my grandfather's brother, my great-uncle Ed. I shall speak more of him later. Stepping into my grandparents' house was like traveling back in time. The wooden kitchen cabinets, unlike the metal updated ones my mother had, were filled with antique kitchen utensils and foodstuffs. Opening the breadbox sitting on the counter in Gramma's house was always a surprise because it usually held more than just bread. Cake, cookies, jelly rolls, and other variety of sweets were usually discovered to my delight, and most of the time, I was able to get permission for something. This ability to con my way to a snack would, of course, have been met with disapproval from my mother, had she known.

Gramma was usually sitting at the kitchen table, which was covered with an oilcloth cover, while she pared, peeled, or prepared something for the next meal. My aunt Virginia would be rocking away in the kitchen rocking chair, listening to her rock and roll music. The house was always warm and inviting, summer or winter, and I much preferred it to my side of the house, which seemed much more spartan and cold.

The proximity of my paternal grandparents gave me, in effect, another set of parents. My father, who worked varied hours, was hardly ever home, it seems. Tough times forced my mother to go to work to supplement the family income by the time we kids were school-age. Probably because of these family dynamics, it seemed natural that my grandparents served as our other parents in absence of our actual parents. I saw them every day, and many times the hours spent with them were as natural as with my own mother and father; the bonding was very real.

The hours I spent with my grandfather both by necessity and by choice eventually led to some problems within the family unit. Analysis in hindsight would indicate that my father became especially envious of the time I spent with my grandfather and that this most likely drove a wedge between us and caused some alienation between my father and grandfather. At the time, however, it just seemed like the normal family tension associated with living in close proximity.

Much was said over the years about the circumstances surrounding my mother and father's courtship and eventual marriage, leading to my being on Earth now, but this story is not about that but about my grandfather as an individual. Let it be known that my mother and grandfather did not always get along; though they tolerated each other's different views on life in general, they did not share much in common. My mother would refer to my grandfather, especially when he was angry, as an "Irish bull" and said his "Irish bull temper" was showing. This was a bit confusing to me because our last name was "Roaf," which is certainly not an Irish derivation but, as I learned later, is German in origin. This is where the story really begins about my grandfather, Chester Warren Roaf.

Grampa, Gramma, and my father in an early studio photo.

Grampa with my father in his arms in front of our house.

Chapter 2
The Family Secret

Being a naturally curious youngster and to some degree having an analytical mind, I questioned the origin of our last name and the constant reference to my grandfather's "Irish" heritage. The only one in the family who would speak to me about it was my mother, and she obviously had learned most of it from my grandmother when she married into the family. In actuality, early in her relationship with my father, she thought his given name was Roafy because that was the nickname his friends used for him at the time. She was probably as curious as I later was about the origin of Roaf as a family name once she and my father decided to marry. The story goes that my grandfather had a different father from his siblings and that he was in fact a Harrington and, therefore, Irish, but his mother was married to Roaf at the time of his birth. This was only partly true, and it took me years of research and genealogical study to truly understand the implications of this family secret. No one would speak outwardly about this situation, except for my grandmother, from whom I later learned bits and pieces but who, I recently became sure, did not know the whole story.

Because of the lack of knowledge, or perhaps because of the knowledge my grandfather did have, he would not speak of his past as a youth or of his origins. It could be that he was embarrassed or that he did not know all of it himself; in any case, I will never understand fully why he would not talk about his past. It was known that he had been orphaned as child and that for years he did not know where his brothers or sisters were because they had been separated as children. Years later, he somehow reconnected with his half-brother Ed and learned of the offspring of another brother, George, whose name had been changed to Holland upon his adoption and who lived in the New York/New Jersey area. He also was aware of one sister, Gladys, who had married and had descendants in the area of western Massachusetts. We occasionally visited these "relatives in Springfield," and the folks from New Jersey visited us. My uncle Ed had married and lived in Cambridge for the latter part of his life and was the only living relative of my grandfather whom I knew as a child. In even later years, when I was a teenager, he actually moved in with my grandparents in the tenement next door.

Uncle Ed was a fascinating character. In the years when he was lost to my grandfather, he allegedly worked in vaudeville and traveled quite a bit. The only pieces of evidence of this I had were the family stories and pictures in an old album that showed him in blackface makeup for some of the vaudeville minstrel acts in which he participated. He was a prolific writer, mainly of poetry, and nearly every holiday for a number of years, his poems were featured on the front page of the Boston papers. I remember reading them when I was young, and from time to time, he would produce old newspaper clippings and letters from presidents that displayed the talent and notoriety of Uncle Ed. Though brothers, Grampa and Uncle Ed looked nothing alike. My research of the family indicated that he and my grandfather's other siblings all were products of different fathers. Though different in so many aspects, they were "family," and my grandfather loved Uncle Ed as much as any person I know.

(Left to right) Uncle Ed and Grandpa in younger days.

Grampa and Uncle Ed a bit older.

To be fair, we knew much more about my grandmother's genealogy, and I have a proud heritage in the Bennett side of the family. I have researched my grandmother's family with some diligence as well, and many are buried in the local cemetery family lots. The history of my grandmother's family dates back to Plymouth Plantation with true English origins, another story that, if I ever have the opportunity, I would like to tell someday as well. For now, I must delve deeper and share more of my relationship with the man I called "Grampa."

Gramma, Grampa, and Dad as a boy.

Chapter 3
The True Origin of Grampa

Hattie M. Bayley was born in September 1859, daughter of David H. and Elvira Bayley, in Newburyport, Massachusetts. At the time of her birth, she had five brothers and sisters, Adeline, Martha, Charles, Caroline, and John. Large families were common in Victorian-era New England, and she herself would have several children, although she would not experience the family life she probably enjoyed as a child. Records indicate she always lived in Massachusetts, at least until the turn of the century, and that her father died when she was the tender age of eleven. It must have been a shock to a girl of such a young age to lose her father and remain in a house with so many siblings. How difficult must it have been for her and her family to survive in nineteenth-century New England with no breadwinner at home? She left school after the death of her father to do housework, and that was the end of her formal education. Was it this early traumatic experience that caused her to hereafter never enjoy the solidarity of a close family life?

At age twenty-two, on November 22, 1881, she married George W. Roaf Jr., but the marriage lasted only six months, and her husband left her. Later records indicate that a boy, Everett Warren Roaf, was born on January 25, 1882. What I discovered next was a surprise and somewhat confusing to me. In the course of my research from the archives in Massachusetts Genealogy, I discovered the following notes from inmate records at the women's prison in Sharon, Massachusetts. I can only gather from these records the obvious facts as they appear and speculate on the circumstances that brought my great-grandmother to be incarcerated at this facility.

> Always lived in Mass. Father died when she was eleven but mother made a home for her children. She did housework when her father died she left school, Her husband left her when she had been married six months. Married at 22. She had been doing housework for a Mr. Barnes of West Newbury (Mass) the past seven years. He is the father of her baby and other man is the father of her boy. Today the boy is with her sister, Mrs Noyes. Expect she will care for him.

The prison census for 1900 lists a baby, Gertrude May Roaf, nine months old, born December 5, 1899, as her child. Further in a section of inmate history is the following:

Hattie Roaf (child Gertrude 3 wks old) Dec 26, 1899. L & L one year. from Newburyport 40 years old married at 22 to George Roaf a baker in Newburyport, only lived with him a few months since then has been doing housework. Two illegitimate children, oldest a boy, eight years old with her sister in Newburyport. Children have different fathers. Released on permit Nov 20, 1900 to go with child to Dedham House.

Her points of contact listed during her incarceration were as follows:

Sister, Mrs Charles S. Noyes of 46 Milk Street, Newburyport, Massachusetts
Marcia Pearson
Mrs Carrie (Noyes)

It is not clear whether the "other man" indicated as the father of her oldest boy was a reference to her husband, George, who had left years earlier, or to someone else not named. Birth records indicate other children over the years and, in some cases, the father responsible. Other than Everett, born to Hattie and George, her husband in 1882, there was Ida Mae Roaf born November 24, 1894, with her father listed as George M. Lomas; his place of birth was listed as Ireland. My grandfather's own birth certificate shows his birth in West Newbury, on February 26, 1896, and his father as Benjamin Harrington, which fits the family legend.

And who was the oldest boy in the custody of her sister? My Uncle Ed's birth date was known to us as May 28, 1890, which is close to the age of the boy mentioned in the prison record. We know Ed was the older brother, but according to family legend, so was my uncle George, who was adopted and taken to New York to live under the name Holland. There is a record of birth for George Holland for June 1895, which fits the timeframe somewhat, with the information passed down in the family verbally. However, the birth of George and that of my grandfather in February 1896 do not correlate. I have not been able to verify Ed's birth record in any of the surrounding towns in Massachusetts for the time period. Finally, my grandfather's purported sister Gladys had a known birth date of October 8, 1908, but I have never substantiated this because it came after the 1900 census and Hattie's incarceration. I have not found any further records of Hattie after she was released to Dedham House for Women and Children in 1900.

It is interesting to note these prison records on a couple of points. Her crime seemed to be "L & L," understood to mean "lewd and lascivious" behavior for a woman of Victorian-era society at the end of the nineteenth century. Had she admitted to other children with different men, would her sentence have been more harsh or the public embarrassment too much? In any case, it is obvious she was not completely honest about her history. Was my great-grandmother a victim of a broken home and limited skills and education, an outcast in a proper society that frowned on such unwed mothers? Had she been the victim of rape by her house master/employer, or was she a coquette using her female charms to survive in a world where her skills and education were limited? I shall never know the answer to these questions, but the birth of my grandfather Chester Warren Roaf is well documented as "illegitimate son," and the father indeed was Benjamin Harrington, originally from Maine. So in line somewhat with the family story, my grandfather was the product of an Irish mother, Bayley, and an Irish father, Harrington. Although his mother was no longer married to Roaf, she continued to use the name and in fact had several other children all with different fathers. The family secret is secret no more, and I understand the embarrassment with which my grandfather may have lived the rest of his life.

It is also interesting to note that her first child with her husband, George W. Roaf, had the middle name Warren, so the father's middle name, with initial W, might have been Warren as well. My grandfather's middle name is also Warren, so I suspect Hattie carried the name and memory on to another child and generation. My brother's given name is Warren after my grandfather. Also, Hattie's two girls of record both had the middle name Mae, or alternate spelling of May. It is somewhat curious but not surprising that my grandparents later gave my aunt Virginia, my father's sister, the middle name May. She was Virginia May Roaf, and I wonder if my grandfather did not have some reason for naming his daughter after two half-sisters whom he may not have even known. It is not uncommon in genealogy to find families reusing and recycling the same name over and over for generations, which makes genealogy all the more difficult.

While examining the family history, I must pause and reflect on the humble beginnings from which my grandfather came. He appeared untainted by the fact that he came from a broken home; he did not see it as an excuse for misbehavior or bad behavior in later life. Yes, there may have been embarrassment, but even without the nurturing environment of the traditional family unit, he modeled values and love for his own family. Psychiatrists and sociologist today state that the human personality is formed by the time a child is five years of age. What then of the formation of character? Can we not choose positive traits while developing as human beings? I submit that my grandfather represents the case where in spite of a lack of early childhood nurturing, he chose to live a life with purpose, and that in itself is encouraging to all of us.

CHAPTER 4
YOUNG LIFE FOR AN ORPHAN

Little is known of Gramps's early life as an orphaned child. I do not know which years he may have spent in an orphanage or when he was separated from his siblings. A 1900 census record indicates his status at four years old as "border" in Littleton, Grafton, New Hampshire. A 1910 census indicates that at age fourteen, he was a "helper" at Fitzhenry Cadillac in Barre, Massachusetts, in Worcester County. Once he told me the story of how he had been drafted and sent to Fort Dix, New Jersey, for induction. I found his Selective Service card among genealogy documents. But the war ended soon after his arrival, so he was told he was not needed and was discharged and free to go home. The trouble was he had been brought there by the military but had no money or means of getting home on his own. When I queried him as to what he did then, he simply said that he went and sat in the orderly room until they tired of him just being there and the military or some officer there arranged for his ticket and sent him on his way home. It was one of many anecdotes attesting to his stubbornness, but also his way of never seeming to worry about things because they always worked out.

We spent many hours spent riding in his old 1955 Dodge pickup truck traveling here and there, especially to the summer camp in Rhode Island. These were times when he would regale me with snippets of his past jobs and some of his work as a youth. He was a jack of all trades, as well as a farmer, and I was often amazed at his knowledge of a variety of subjects. He had retired from the Whitin Machine Works Company, where he had worked in the shops as some sort of machine operator. Whitin Machine played an integral part in producing machinery of all types, especially during World War II. I am not certain as to my grandfather's true job or skill set because I always saw him as a small dirt farmer, on what we referred to as a "truck farm," where most everything was done by hand or with small machines.

His ability to fix things and sheer general knowledge amazed me. I often wondered how one person had come to know so much about so many different things. It didn't seem like there was a subject Grampa didn't know something about. I believe his knowledge came from a lifetime of toil and hard work. I gathered he had worked countless jobs as a youth, including for a while one as a postal carrier, when he carried a small "belly gun," a small pistol of small caliber and little accuracy, for personal protection; it is even worse than a "Saturday night special" and very cheaply made. He also told me how he had worked on the large oil storage tanks they were building in the port of Providence, Rhode Island, long ago. Other than these few interceding jobs, he had spent most of his time working on farms and farming his own land after marrying my grandmother in November 1918 (their fiftieth golden wedding anniversary in 1968 was especially memorable for me, and the 8 mm film of it is still in my parents' possession).

Grampa told me how he had married my grandmother with only two dollars in his pocket, which he paid to the preacher, and he took his bride home in the horse and buggy to live at that time in a house in Sutton. My grandmother had lived on a farm in Sutton, Massachusetts, and after her father died, she had invested her portion of her inheritance in some land in the southeast portion of Sutton, a subset town of Manchaug, where she bought several acres and the house I grew up in with my grandparents living next door. My grandfather, in addition to his day job at the shop, worked a fairly large garden by himself, with me serving, of course, as his free labor as I grew older. Neither my sister nor my younger brother ever spent the time in contact with the soil that I did working with and for Grampa. The rule was if you expected to eat, you were expected to work.

(Left to right) Aunt Edith, Grampa,
Gramma and Dad as a boy.

Chapter 5
The 1950s

My grandfather was born in 1896, my grandmother was born in 1900, and I came along a half-century later in 1950. I was the first and the oldest grandchild on both sides of my family, but my proximity to Grampa and Gramma allowed them to dote on me much more. My maternal grandmother and grandfather, who were divorced, were French, so the appropriate terms for them were Memé and Pepé, so there was never any confusion.

My grampa loved his dogs, and there were in fact generations of dogs named "Skippy." The first Skippy was a two-toned tan-colored German shepherd who protected me fearlessly while I was still in the baby carriage. I have seen photographs and films of this dog, along with the stories I heard, so I know this was indeed Gramps's and my best friend. Grampa always owned a dog and almost always a German shepherd, although none had the sweet disposition of the first Skippy. I had my own dog as well, a small cocker-beagle mix, black as night, named Sparky, whom my father brought home to me when she and I were both two weeks old. We grew up together, and she died at fifteen when I was in high school. That dog would run alongside Grampa's pickup when he went to the top of the hill where the garden was and spend the entire time up there with my grandfather and me; she was in effect his other dog. She would hunt out and kill woodchucks as big as she was from time to time, which always amazed me because I do not recall her ever killing anything else or ever showing any signs of aggression toward any other creature.

Grampa always had a love for animals, especially dogs, even though there were always cats too, and when I was really young, we had ducks, chickens, and cows for milking, and for a while, Grampa even had some hogs. As I grew older and my father and Gramps spent full days working away from home, the hogs, chickens, and ducks went away, but for fresh whole milk, we had our cow Blossom, whom Grampa milked twice a day for as long as I remember and for as long as he was capable. In addition, he was busy with tending the garden and working a full-time job until he retired at sixty-five from the shop. Occasionally, he would have Blossom inseminated, and we would have a calf to raise, always named "Buttercup." Grampa would raise the calf and sell him or her off for extra money from time to time. He recycled animal names like most people recycled given names, and I never understood that.

Grampa, Gramma, and first "Skippy."

Few people today have any idea of the amount of work, even on a small farm, that is required to produce enough vegetables for the family to eat and sell; to keep a cow, which means milking and feeding hay and grain; to manage all the other upkeep to house and buildings; to maintain and fix fences; to bring in hay for the winter; and to cut, split, and stack wood for the stove. We burned kerosene oil in our furnace in our side of the house. It was my job to fill the small tank behind the stove from the fifty-gallon drums we kept in the cellar. My grandparents burned wood for heat and cooking the whole time I lived there, until I left home after high school.

Grampa, Dad behind the cow, and Aunt Virginia on the cow!

"We were poor, but didn't know it at the time." That was the conclusion my brother drew years later. I would not have considered us below middle class, compared to what I saw the other kids at school had. In our neighborhood, we were all about the same. The other kids had parents who worked in the mills or other blue-collar professions. There was a lot of doing without in those days, but because everyone else was doing without too, it seemed normal. It began to dawn on us years later that maybe we did have a bit less than some of the other families. My father earned near minimum wage most of his life. Much of our food was supplemented from the garden. The old house had few amenities such as central heating or hot running water. We obtained our water directly from a well. Any hot water we needed for baths was heated on the stove in pans and carried upstairs to the tub. Even my father shaved by heating water in a teakettle first and pouring it into the sink. This was the reality I grew up with all the way through high school. It was only after I left home that my parents "modernized" by putting in central heating and buying my mother a clothes dryer.

Materialism today seems to be the all-important factor for happiness to many people. Who was it who said, "The person who dies with the most toys wins"? Growing up in a world where not everything comes so easily taught me frugality and appreciation for what possessions I might own. Like my grandparents who grew up in a world with even less in the way of possessions than we had, for me the distinction between wants and needs is very clear. Upon reflection, I do not seek pity or feel regret that I did not have all the things others had. No, I am thankful that the experience taught me the importance of values beyond physical objects—the values of frugality, preparation, saving, and honesty and the joy that comes with independence.

CHAPTER 6
WORK HARD AT WHATEVER YOU DO

The idea that you should work hard at whatever you do is expressed in Ecclesiastes 9:10. Quote: Whatever your hand finds to do, do it with might...

I have split and stacked my share of wood in my day. What amazes me even now is my grandfather's expertise at this task and the relative strength it took for him. Later in my own life, when splitting wood by hand, I would use a maul ax, which is weighted to perhaps sixteen pounds and makes splitting wood fairly easy if you know what you are doing. One must learn to "read" the grain of the wood, and I can split most logs with one chop, or if it is a large oak wheel off a trunk of hard oak, I can split it with three whacks. My grandfather split wood his whole life with a regular wood ax, not significantly weighted as a maul ax, and how he could split a log with one whack was amazing to watch. Usually my father and my uncle Wilmer would help with the annual filling of the wood shed with cut wood, but it was my grampa who split it all, by hand, every day with just an ax.

Another annual, and sometimes semiannual, task was bringing in the hay to dry in the loft and provide feed for the cow all winter. Gramps would hire someone to cut the fields, and he would rake the hay by hand with an old doweled wooden rake into wind-rows. Then, a hired man with a baling machine would come and bale the hay and leave it in the field. That was the only machine assist we had. Haying time was exciting for me because I got to work with the "men" of the family. Usually, it was Grampa; Uncle Wilmer (who was married to my grandmother's sister Edith, my great-aunt); another relative of the Bennetts named Jumbo, a cousin somehow to my gramma; and occasionally my own father when he was not working. I was but a boy, and there were only so many hooks available to grab the bales, so I had to handle them by the baling string. With just the pickup truck, we would go out to the fields, pick up the bales, and throw them on the truck, and Uncle Wilmer would stack them high over the cab while Gramps drove the truck. A not quite fully dried bale of hay can weigh between forty and fifty pounds, so it was great work for a skinny lad as I was, but the camaraderie of working together and the feeling of accomplishment at day's end was something I'll never forget.

I do not recall Grampa being ill a day of his life. The pictures I saw of him when he was younger showed a rather thin man who obviously loved to swim. My memory of him was much older with powerful arms and some girth. I remember watching him handle the monster "walk behind" tractor as he plowed the fields. He appeared to manhandle the machine by sheer force and strong will as the drive wheels and tines tried to go their own way. I could easily imagine him behind a mule doing the same thing as a young man. I was fairly fit and an athletic seventeen-year-old before I could finally beat him at arm wrestling; he would have been seventy-one at that time.

When Grampa would bring in the fresh milk from the cow, he would run it through the "separator" in his kitchen. This was a machine that separated some of the rich cream from the whole milk. I remember helping Gramps put together a series of metal funnel-like cones that fit into the machine for operation. He always allowed me to somehow feel useful and gave me jobs to do, unpaid except for the sheer joy of learning from and being with him.

CHAPTER 7
WORKING AND LEARNING
IN THE GARDEN

Even now, when spring days warm the soil, and the air feels fresh, I get the urge to plunge my hands once again into the rich Earth and plant seeds with great anticipation. Gramps always said he had dirt in his blood and professed on more than one occasion how proud he was to be a farmer. Although he had other jobs and you might say another formal profession, he was first and foremost a farmer. It was not just a job or occupation but a way of life; it was in fact his state of being.

There are many things that determine a good farmer, and production is certainly one measure. It was amazing that on little less than two acres, we produced enough to feed two nuclear family units of nine people and still had plenty to sell, and yes, much was also given away at times. We produced enough potatoes alone to last the family the entire winter. My grandfather had a reputation for the sweetest corn and the most luscious strawberries, never mind the tomatoes, squash, peppers, and raspberries he also sold. Yellow beans, green beans, asparagus, rhubarb—we had it all, and we supplied most of the town kids with their jack-o'-lantern pumpkins as well as many a pumpkin pie at Thanksgiving. As mentioned, he sold the extra produce for income and to offset his farming costs, which he did off the back of his pickup truck all around the area. He had a proper scale to weigh out the vegetables by the pound, and I had my first lessons in salesmanship, customer service, and entrepreneurial activity. Gramps always gave "a little over" in weight for what was paid, and the corn was always a "baker's dozen" of thirteen ears for the price of twelve. He not only had quality produce, but he also had customers always ready to repeat the sale. I don't believe he ever made any real profit from the vegetables if you really figured all his costs and labor, but it helped his cash flow at times, and everyone around the area knew my grandfather personally. My role did not end with these trips accompanying my grandfather. I often would load up my bicycle basket and go around the entire town selling the produce from either my grandfather's garden or mostly my father's garden. I was a chip off the old block, as everyone came to say of "the Roaf boy" or Chester Roaf's grandson. By the way, I always turned over all the money and remember never keeping any for myself. The rule in the family was everyone contributed to the household for the roof over our heads and the food in our mouths.

Before I had my own paper route, the only opportunity I had to make my own money from the family enterprise was during strawberry season. My grandfather would pay me ten cents a quart for every quart I would pick. We started early in the cooler morning hours before the dew was even off the plants. It was sore-knees, backbreaking, hot work to pick twenty quarts to earn two dollars! The season usually came just before the traveling carnival came to town, and that was how I earned my spending money. Grampa was also very fastidious about picking "clean" in the patch and about being sure I picked only the ripe ones and didn't squish them too much. Gramma always picked them over before sale, even my grandpa's pickings, so the best went for sale, and the rest we ate at home. I could also eat as many as I wanted while picking, but eating slows you down, and it takes longer to fill your basket.

It was well known that my grandfather raised the biggest, juiciest, sweetest strawberries in the area. His strawberry crop brought in a good amount of money, and though the patch was relatively small scale, it produced a great amount of surplus strawberries to sell. Part of the credit for this grand production could be given to the fact that my grampa was an apiarist—a beekeeper—and like everything else, he taught me about beekeeping as I accompanied him to the hives. The whole garden, as well as the strawberries, received much benefit from the pollination work of his bees. I was so fascinated with bees from the work with Gramps that I did my high school science project on beekeeping one year and received honorable mention. Grampa knew a lot about bees, and for a while, one of his proudest times was serving as president of the Worcester County Beekeepers Association, a title often mentioned when the newspapers would write of him and accomplishments on his little farm. Again, I was usually by his side when we visited his hives out back of our house or when he serviced hives he had lent out to a couple families for their gardens. Whether it was feeding the bees during cold weather or taking the honey off or treating them for the disease of foul brood, I was usually somewhere around learning in amazement and wondering who had taught this man so much about everything he did. I do not even know how long my grandfather attended a normal school or if he in fact ever "graduated" from some school. I doubt he ever did. Neither he nor anyone else ever indicated anything to me of his formal academic education. He had fairly nice, legible cursive handwriting, so I assume he learned it somewhere, and he certainly could figure his numbers and measure with tools. He could read, but he was not a reader, as I recall.

Grampa with a live bee super.

Chapter 8
Lessons Learned

He taught me how to prepare soil and plant and space different crops appropriately, keeping the weeds at bay and harvesting and planting in rotation so that the soil was replenished. Along with the agricultural lessons came other subjects and lessons for life, including what birds would sing in the morning and which to listen for at night and how to read the weather clouds and listen to the katydid chirp to tell the temperature on a hot day. I learned about tools and also how to tell a bad weed or plant from a good one in the woods. How many readers of this will have picked huckleberries and tasted their minty flavor or knew the benefits of royal jelly before the advent of health food stores? There was no limit, it seemed, to his worldly knowledge or knowledge of any subject matter at hand.

If I were to complain about getting my hands dirty because I had touched some of the "soup" we mixed of cow manure, water, and fertilizer for the tomato plants, he would harangue me with, "You'll eat a peck of dirt before you die, boy!" One of the most forcible lessons came to me on a day when we were out fixing the barbed-wire fence that encircled the cow pasture where we kept Blossom. That cow was a natural bovine Houdini if ever God made one. If there was a slight break in the fence anywhere, she would get loose and run around town, which of course terrorized the local residents. She even learned how to place her head between the sliding cross poles at the gate and work the poles to one side and get free. We had to place barbed wire across the gate to prevent her from breaking out that way. Other times she managed to jump a fence, *uphill*, over barbed wire! I have heard of jumping horses but not like that cow could jump! There were often calls when someone had seen our cow and caught her, if they were brave enough, and tied her to the flagpole at the town common. Going to retrieve the cow with Grampa when she got out was great fun for me, and he seemed to enjoy the spectacle of leading her back home by the road, a one-man, one-cow parade, with all the neighbors hiding behind their screen doors as Gramps led old Blossom down the center of the street. Of course, he would always stop when he knew they were looking and ask Blossom for "a kiss," and the cow would oblige him with a big lick of her tongue across his face to the sounds of laughter and revulsion from the onlookers. I could tell by his grin and the twinkle in his eye that he enjoyed every minute of his notoriety.

Grampa with a cow that looked like our Blossom.

As I was saying, he reprimanded me fairly severely one day. We had been trudging deep within the pine woods where the truck could not go, carrying a bucket of nails, hammer, barbed wire, and fence posts to look for breaks in the fence line and repair them. I was still a scrawny, or lanky, lad, and I was carrying the fence posts, three on each shoulder, cut in triangle-shaped lengths. As I struggled to balance their weight, they were digging grooves into my shoulders. After stumbling along the uneven path for a time and growing tired, my shoulders hurting, I exclaimed the most unforgivable: something to the effect of "Grampa, I can't …" Well, I don't even recall finishing the sentence. The lecture that followed was one about how there was no such word as "can't" and how if I set my mind to it, I could do most anything. That was the gist of it anyway, and maybe I had been complaining for a while, and he had heard enough. I am not saying he was mean about it, and I don't recall that he said it in anger, but he communicated the message in such a forceful manner that I never forgot it and remember to this day that there is no such word as "can't," at least not in my grandfather's vocabulary.

The only time my grandfather brought me to tears was during an incident of disrespect. I was with my grandparents and a neighbor lady at our place in Rhode Island, and this lady was speaking of some subject I do not even recall. I remember the incident outcome because it affected me so deeply and personally. The lady had paused in her discourse to ask me a question, and I exclaimed quite forcefully, "You're a liar," which was the thought on my mind at that moment. The air was dead still for a couple of seconds as the effect of what I had just done sank in. My grandmother, aghast at my response, could only say my name in great disappointment and anger. Grampa began to lay in to me in no uncertain terms about being respectful to my elders and never saying such a thing to an adult again; he made me apologize to the lady. I was so heartbroken and devastated, not only from the embarrassment but also because I had disappointed my grandparents so much. I never again spoke disrespectfully to my elders.

CHAPTER 9
SUMMERS AT THE OCEAN

My grandparents owned a cottage in Greenwich, Rhode Island, that they used each summer to be near the ocean. I say "owned" because allegedly they owned the building that was located in a campground where one could lease the land but never own it under the original terms. It was a confusing setup and was designed in the days when it allowed the "poor people" to have access to the beach and ocean, in an area that could never be sold off to developers or the very wealthy. The "camp," as we referred to it, was nothing like you would imagine. It looked to be a hastily built structure, constructed when zoning and building codes were nonexistent, probably in the 1930s. Interior walls were one board thick, with no insulation, sheetrock, or wallpaper, just painted boards that, in places, you could see between into the other room. To say it was rustic was giving it even more elaborateness than it deserved. There were not glass windows anywhere, but instead shutters that covered screens, and there was no means of heating the space, save the cook stove on an atypical spring or fall night when the weather could be still be quite cool or rainy. It had running cold water and an indoor toilet, but that was the extent of amenities. There was not even a television unless you hauled one down and used rabbit ears to get a snowy picture of channel 12 out of Providence, Rhode Island. You would think a child would be bored to death in such a place, but on the contrary, the camp was a wonderful place, and I very much enjoyed my times there as a youth!

My grandparents had owned the camp since my father was a mere boy himself. Born in 1927, he was sickly as a youth, and the doctor's prescription for his health was that his parents "take him to the ocean where the salt air will do him good!" So my grandparents found the camp, and it stayed in the family, leased each year for a reasonable fee until after my grandmother died. Probably the greatest thing about those times was that I was out from the restrictions of my own parents; however, do not think that my grandmother did not keep a close eye on me and have her own set of rules. It seemed to me, however, that I was freer to roam and to do such things as eating corn flakes straight out of the cereal box, which I never would have done at home.

Grampa, Aunt Edith, and my father
as a young boy at the ocean.

I would often go to the camp for a week or so, which I'm sure gave my mother a respite during the summer, and I either rode down with my grandmother or traveled on Friday night with Grampa in the truck. He was still working a regular job then, so he often would travel down only for the weekends, unless it was vacation time, but my grandmother would stay through the week until she had to return to see her doctor, which was quite often. It was on these trips with my grandfather that we had wonderful times. I don't believe the truck even had an AM radio in those days, so we would talk, or he would sing a funny ditty of a song. I never knew whether he was making up a song or it was a real song. He would suddenly burst out singing something like "Old Dan Yeller was a very funny fella, with his feet upstairs and his head down cellar!" Without the new highways, it was about a two-hour trip in those days, on two-lane roads through a number of small New England towns, but I knew every turn and every route number. I remember how pleased I was to amaze my gramps with my memory of the long trip. I would act as navigator and tell him each turn to make along the way. It was a game we both enjoyed and served to increase my memory skill and attention span. Perhaps Grampa was giving me another lesson I wasn't aware of at the time.

Chapter 10
The Quahog King

The camp was a recreational paradise for me. When Grampa was down, he would always take me to dig for quahogs, which we called "quahoggin." Quahogs were unlike long-neck clams that are dug in the mud at low tide. Quahogs were large, rounded edible clams of the Atlantic coast of North America, also called hard clams or hard-shelled clams. They were great steamed, in New England clam chowder, and in clam cakes (deep-fried dough similar to Southern hush puppies but not made with cornmeal), and in fact we even had them in pancakes for breakfast! My gramps would eat them raw, like people eat oysters, but I could never bring myself to do that myself. We would dig them by the bushel full while standing in the water, sometimes up to my grandfather's chest, and some people dug them from boats in deeper water with longer mandible-type rakes.

Now, Grampa was a master at digging quahogs and taught me how to drag the rake along the bottom until "the bell would ring," as he put it, meaning you could feel the sensation of the clam under the rake. The rake was simply a potato hook with wire mesh affixed across the back of the tines to basket the clams. There was an art to getting just under the clam, raking it to the top of the mud, and with a flip of your wrist, flipping the rake over to bring up the clams. A regular bushel basket with an inner tube around it would be tied to your waist, where you would place the clams until you returned to the beach and had to carry the basket home. This was hard work, and you were in the water, starting at low tide, for hours and hours. This, I thought, was great fun!

Occasionally, sand sharks would swim by in the shallow water, and I would spot them and jump after them. They were about two feet long and harmless for all intents and purposes but, I'm sure, capable of biting if they wanted. The other creature that was common in these waters was the horseshoe crab, a relic from the true dinosaur era that you probably only see now in aquariums. Most of the time, I found them dead where they had washed up on the beach and were caught at low tide, but occasionally Grampa also would bring one up on the rake while digging quahogs. My grandfather appreciated nature and recognized the natural order of life, and we, like respectful hunters and fishermen, took only what we knew we would eat and within the legal size limits. I never feared these creatures, and an admission of fear certainly would have brought comment from Grampa.

The Quahog King.

A couple of times, we went fishing in his boat, which was not much more than an ocean skiff; it was about fourteen feet long, built of sturdy wood, and a bit deeper than a freshwater rowboat. We took it to his secret place for digging clams off of an island once, and Gramma had come along, so we had a day of it with a picnic lunch.

One day, while I was fishing with Grampa and Uncle Wilmer, the experience became a bit harrowing. They both fished with large sea fishing poles and casting reels while I fished with a handline. If you have ever seen the movie *Old Man and the Sea* with Spencer Tracy or read the book you would know exactly the kind of handline I mean. I grasped the line in the palm of my hand until I could feel the tug of the fish, and then, in a hand-over-hand motion, pulled the fish from the depths into the boat. We would fish for flounder, or blues, or any type of "good" fish, but we also caught blowfish (or porcupine fish, as they are sometimes known), sand sharks, and sea robins, another type of scavenger fish.

On the way in after several hours, and probably much too far out to sea for such a small boat, a storm blew up, and the seas got really rough. Dark, heavy clouds formed, and we could sense the rain coming as the temperature dropped. The swells became larger and larger, mountainous from the perspective of a small boy like me. I sensed at the time that my gramps and uncle may have been worried, especially when the boat would drop between the swells, and I could not see anything but sky and water. The sound from the twenty-five-horsepower Johnson motor droned on, pushing the craft through the swells as ocean spray splashed our faces with each wave. I was young, not more than nine or ten at the time, but I never felt afraid because I knew I was with my grampa, and he would take care of me. If my mother only knew! I don't think that was a story I ever shared.

CHAPTER 11
LEARNING TO SWIM

Most young country boys of my time learned a lot from their grandfathers, like the feeling of a clutch and shifting a three-speed on the column in the pickup truck, and I was no exception. Backing the truck in and out of the short driveway was the beginning of my driving experience, and the fact that Gramps trusted me to do it was the greatest confidence builder. I would also have to credit Grampa with teaching me how to swim, but it wasn't that he taught me the mechanics of swimming so much as he gave the confidence to know I could swim.

The boat he had at the oceanfront was anchored in the water not far from shore. Although it may seem completely naive today, people were principled and more honest back then, so the boat was not secured except that it was tied to anchor rope with a float to mark the spot, left totally in the open with no cover or security. It was anchored far enough out that it would ride the tides without becoming beached at low tide, so you had to either wade out to it or swim to it, depending on the tide. One day after a night of rain, Grampa took me with him to "bail out the boat," to remove all the rainwater that had accumulated so that the boat would not sink from more rain. This was usually done with the efficient means of a bent coffee can (so you could get in the corners) and hours of hand bailing.

This day, we waded out to the boat, which was in the water almost over my head and pretty well up to the chest of my grandfather. Because he was in his sixties and carried quite a belly, he suggested to me that he was not nimble enough to climb in the boat in such deep water and boosted me into the boat to begin the bailing while he watched. Now the tide had turned, and it was going to high tide on its six-hour cycle, so as the tide continued to rise and the water became deeper, he had to move toward shore, not being able to stand by the boat. I continued to bail, and when I finally finished, my gramps was perhaps halfway between the boat and the beach several yards away. I yelled to him, "Okay, Grampa, I'm done—come and get me!" I thought I could hold on to his back as he swam me back to shore. I knew the water was now over my head near the boat, and there I was, knowing I could not yet swim. I had been shown the mechanics of swimming, the crawling motion of the arms and legs, and I desperately would have liked to swim, but I always seemed to sink like a rock, which brought panic and usually a mouthful of water. I loved the water and would spend hours at the beach with my grandmother, playing in the surf or simply floating in my inner tube on which my gramps had actually painted my name so that I wouldn't lose it. I would stay in the water until my grandmother insisted that I come out because, as she put it, my "lips were turning blue," a condition she was sure indicated hypothermia. But to be over my head in deep water was another matter, even though I desperately wanted to learn to swim.

Grampa's response to my request for rescue was immediately disconcerting if not disappointing: "Sorry," he said, "I can't reach you. You will just have to swim it from there." I couldn't believe my ears, but I knew when he was serious and that he wasn't going to rescue me. I didn't panic but thought to myself that if Grampa believed I could do it, then I guess I'd better at least try. I took a breath and jumped out of the boat into the deep water and began furiously moving my arms and legs as fast as I could, trying and hoping to propel myself toward shallow water. My grandfather just stood there and stoically watched. I often wonder if this was all done with calculation and trickery on his part or happened by pure chance. Needless to say, I didn't drown, and my foot finally touched the bottom where I could stand, at which point I shouted, "I did it! Grampa, I actually swam on my own!" My grampa just looked at me knowingly. It was not that I couldn't swim, but to that point, I had not found the confidence in myself. That is a lesson I remembered and applied later in life as well. Sometimes you just have to have the confidence to jump in, even when the situation is over your head, and rely on your instinct, talent, and natural ability to save yourself.

CHAPTER 12
SOLAR SHOWER IN THE SIXTIES

Anyone who has spent time swimming in saltwater knows that the salt drying on your skin is sticky, and when you add the residual sand, the entire feeling can be quite uncomfortable. Having no bathtubs or shower at the camp meant old-fashioned sponge baths or whatever means possible to freshen up. I told you the camp was primitive and without amenities! Upon returning from a day at the beach, I had an established ritual where my grandmother would fill a dish basin with cold tap water and commence dousing me from head to foot while I stood outside the door. Maybe two or three basins full would sufficiently allow the salt to be washed from my person before I would dry off and go in to change out of my wet swim trunks. Boy, was that water ever cold, but I never complained that I remember. It felt so good not to feel sticky all over. This happened for several years until my grandfather could not stand to see me suffer any longer. He obtained an old water tank from someplace, or a close facsimile to one, and placed it on the top of the storage shed behind the camp, where we kept all the beach gear. He then constructed a wooden platform alongside the building and plumbed a shower from the tank on the roof to the shower head. No hiring a plumber, no building codes or permits, just ingenuity, time, and scrap materials. He painted the tank with black paint so that the water in the tank would heat from the sun all day, and voila, a solar-heated shower that would last at least a few minutes. You had to be wary if you were second or third in line to use the shower, though, because you would be back to my cold-water experience of several years. My grandfather would tell people later that he just got tired of seeing me take my cold-water basin baths. It was always a humorous story to tell for him. The ingenuity of the man and his skills continued to amaze me for many years.

Another project that warrants mention was the outdoor fireplace, as I called it. In the days before barbecue grills and the popularity of all the grilling equipment one can purchase today, people still enjoyed cookouts as a favorite summer activity. I even remember us hosting a "New England Shore Dinner" or clambake in our backyard in Massachusetts, many miles from the ocean. The summer camp was a perfect place for such a cookout, with our picnic table, also built by my grandfather, under the tall shade trees. With the assistance of some cousins from my grandmother's side of the family for labor, my grandfather constructed an all-stone fire pit, complete with rebar on which to place kettles and pans above the fire. It had a chimney to carry off the smoke and looked like a giant stone chair or throne in shape. This was all accomplished without the aid of drawings, a written plan, or special tools, just ingenuity and hard labor to carry and set the large stones. It was quite a monstrosity to see, but I will bet it is still standing, as formidable a structure as it was.

The outside fireplace. That is me on the lower left. I could not have been more than six or seven years old at the time. Standing are Jumbo Bennett, Grampa, and Kenny Bennett. The Bennetts were my grandmother's side of the family.

Chapter 13
Birds on the Roof

The camp, as I previously described, was a fairly rustic structure built decades ago without modern conveniences or building codes for construction. It had a tar-paper roof and may have had some metal under the paper, though I don't really know. But I had seen my gramps, with help, repair roof leaks over the years with the rolls of tar paper and the hot, smelly, sticky, gooey tar that cooled and patched the leaks wherever they were. There was no insulation, and the roof was probably one board thick, so if even an acorn fell on the roof, you could hear it hit and bounce around.

One evening, when I was tucked in my bed with heavy blankets holding me down and wrapped around me like a cocoon, because Gramma was always afraid I would "catch a death of cold," I heard my grandparents talking on the other side of the shared wall as they lay in bed. "Listen to that!" I heard my grandfather say. "You can hear the birds walking on the roof." I listened to the quiet, both for the birds and to hear my gramma's response.

After a pause, I heard Gramma chuckle and say, "Those aren't birds, Chester. It's raining. That's the rain on the roof!"

"Oh, sounds just like birds walking on the roof to me," Grampa said.

I smiled as I listened to the noise again, and it *did* sound like birds walking on the roof! It was one of the funniest conversations I have ever heard. It was, after all, a matter of perception, and things are not always as they appear or sound. Imagination is also a wonderful thing, and oh how I loved listening to the rain after that and thinking, *It could be birds walking on the roof,* and smiling as I fell to sleep.

CHAPTER 14
PANCAKES FOR BREAKFAST

My grandmother may not have been the best cook in the world, as grand cooking goes, but she cooked a lot—pies and cakes as well as hearty meals because there was no fear of cholesterol or obesity back then for hardworking country folk. She cooked the old-fashioned way, with lard, or bacon grease, or butter. Her pie crust could be heavy enough for a doorstop, but it all tasted good. I don't know what their cholesterol or blood pressure levels were. The whole family carried extra weight (except me at the time, but I have followed the tradition since), but both my grandparents lived well into their eighties.

My grandfather loved his food, and the variety of what he ate was amazing. Most of the time, it was very simple fare, and nothing would go to waste. Many times I watched him eat a lunch of blueberries and milk or graham crackers and milk, strawberries, leftovers, or whatever was available and in season. He loved his coffee "strong enough to stand a spoon up in it." The coffee, percolated on a wood stove, was great when fresh, but it could approach the consistency of lacquer if left too long or reheated later in the day. Grampa would actually eat pickled pigs' feet and seemed to enjoy them! There were many food items that I am glad to say I never could bring myself to put in my mouth, but Gramps did.

After watching my grandmother cook meal after sumptuous meal, I thought that I would show my appreciation and cook breakfast for them one morning. I could not have been more than seven or eight years old at the time so this was a big undertaking for just a small lad. My grandfather and I loved pancakes, or flapjacks, which was much more fun to say, and everyone else liked them too. Because they were normally early risers, I had to get up extra early and be very, very quiet so that I could prepare the surprise. I mixed the batter perfectly, just like my grandmother had, and lit the gas stove and obtained one of the big, heavy cast-iron skillets that hung on the wall. I poured the batter in the pan and waited for the batter to bubble, the sign that it was time to turn over the mixture and make my first pancake. Then something went terribly wrong! I tried to flip the pancake, but it was stuck to the pan, and try as I might, I could not flip it without the pancake tearing apart and continuing to overcook in a gooey blackened mess. I removed the skillet pan from the heat and grabbed another pan off the wall. Same thing. I tried perhaps three different pans with the same gooey results until the noise, smell of burned batter, or perhaps some smoke awakened my grandmother, who came into the kitchen to see what the fuss was all about. I was nearly in tears, frustrated and disappointed that my surprise had failed miserably, and I didn't know if I was in big trouble or not. I explained my attempt through a high frustrated voice, but my gramma did not appear angry at all. She just chuckled and told me, if you haven't already guessed my mistake, that I had forgotten to grease the pan first! I think they appreciated my good intentions, and she rescued the breakfast by making the pancakes that morning, and everything was fine. They would laugh about my attempt at making pancakes for years to come, and I'm sure it was a sweet memory for them. I am just glad that my grandparents were both tolerant and forgiving of a lad who made mistakes. They allowed me to be adventurous and to learn, building my confidence instead of being critical of everything I did.

CHAPTER 15
A ROOT BEER FOR ME

Traveling with Gramps, whether at the camp or around our hometown, was always an experience somehow. I don't think that I have ever seen a person swell so much with pride as when he introduced me to one of his friends or to a stranger with, "And that's my grandson!" He always said it with such pride and love that I was almost always embarrassed. No one has ever said the words "I love you" with more pronouncement or feeling than my grampa did with his introductions of me.

Now, my family were pretty much teetotalers, given that we were pretty good Methodists, but my grampa did like an occasional beer, wine on holidays, or on even more rare occasion, a stronger drink. I would see him sometimes at Thanksgiving or Christmas quite merry from the port wine or, believe it or not, Manischewitz grape wine, though he was not Jewish or kosher, of course, and purchased the wine for the price more than the taste; it was sort of like Welch's grape juice with a kick. I never saw him really inebriated or drunk, so I do not wish for the reader to get the wrong impression. Others in the family, however, did overindulge at times, so I knew when I was looking at someone who was over the limit even as a child. Whether these relatives, remaining nameless, had a serious drinking problem, I do not judge, even now, and it was not a problem for me, and I did not love them any less for it.

Grampa would from time to time "have to see a man about a horse," which was his euphemism for getting a drink or stopping off at a bar. Yes, I did accompany him on these excursions because I was with him whenever possible. Taking a child of nine or ten to sit in a bar may not seem politically correct or even may be considered child abuse by some uptight standards of today, but in the late 1950s and '60s, this was not enough to raise an eyebrow. I would sit on a stool next to my grampa, and he would order a beer and a "root beer for my grandson," and we would drink a cold one and then leave. We did not sit for hours, and he never misbehaved in any way; he was just being a man and enjoying the company of his grandson. I, of course, felt very adult. If I learned anything from these experiences, it was that there is nothing wrong with being a male, being a man, and drinking was not evil and did not have to become a crutch for weakness. I learned that drinking, like anything else, in moderation or minimally, is a social ritual that does not vilify a person. Actions speak louder than words, and my grandfather did not have to preach to me about over-imbibing and the dangers of intoxication.

"Take my picture!" Grampa with a bottle of beer.

CHAPTER 16
A TOAST TO THE ANCESTORS

Another memorable incident took place much later in my life; in fact, I believe I was already in the military and was of drinking age. I had come home on leave, and quite often on these visits, my grandfather and I would enjoy sitting at the kitchen table and having a beer with some hard, sharp cheddar cheese. We would talk of nothing in particular and just enjoy each other's company and visit. My grampa was not a deep person interested in discussing real philosophy, for example, but I absorbed a lot from him that was significant. On this one occasion, rather than a beer he announced that he had been saving something for me. He brought out an old, and I mean old, bottle of bourbon, the brand of which I did not recognize and do not remember. It had belonged, he said, to my great-grandfather Bennett, which you might recall was the maiden name of my grandmother. My great-grandfather Bennett, it seems, did have a notion for his whiskey, in moderation of course, and this bottle had been found with just about two shots left in the bottom. Grampa knew of my appreciation for nostalgia and my ancestors because I had often queried about them and always listened as he explained to me about "the old days" or old ways and old things. He was, as I previously indicated, very guarded about his own beginnings, but he shared with relish any stories of others in the family. He ceremoniously poured the brown liquid into two glasses, and we decided to drink the very last remaining ancient whiskey by toasting my great-grandfather and my ancestors. I whiffed at the glass, drawing in the musty aroma of years ago, and tried to savor the experience with all my senses. The taste as I sipped down the liquid is but faint now in my memory. It had a slight burn but was smooth at the same time, and as far as whiskeys go, it was probably not of the highest quality available. But although I have tasted many fine whiskeys since, none has the same memory, importance, or significance as that toast shared with my grampa. Just the fact that he thought to save it and drink it with me will always stay with me as testimony to the respect and admiration we shared.

Chapter 17
Winters in New England

As you might imagine, the winter months in New England were long and cold, with short days; long, dark nights; and plenty of weather. Some memories, however, are very warm, especially of my grandparents' house. Instead of "over the river and through the woods," my grandparents were a step or two out the back door and into their house, where instantly you were transported back in time a couple of decades. The calendar may have indicated that it was the sixties, but my mother's side of the house reflected fifties decor down to the patterned kitchen chrome table and linoleum floors, and my grandparents' house was a decade or two earlier, less updated, with heavy wood seemingly taking over the furniture. The chairs were wood, and my grampa's favorite chair was big and stuffed; it was so comfortable that sitting in it had the effect of lowering your blood pressure by ten points. There was an exquisite Tiffany floor lamp next to his chair, which was also near the window so that when he sat, he could look out and check the window thermometer. When you stepped into the kitchen, the acrid smell of the wood stove filled your nostrils, and the heat from the fire, making the room at least twenty degrees warmer than my parents' house, would hit you full in the face. Advanced in years, my grandparents, like other elder folks, were always feeling cold. Even with the heat, my grandmother would have a shawl or sweater on, and admittedly, there were times that I could stand it for only so long and would have to retreat back to my side or outside to the cold crisp air in order to breathe.

More often than not, in the evening hours I would visit them, still early by the clock, though after dark, because they believed in going early to bed and rose earlier than any of us next door. It was on evenings like this that I would find my grandfather watching his favorite television show, *The Real McCoys.* The character Grandpa Amos, played by the great actor Walter Brennan, was the embodiment and incarnation of my own grandfather, though Grampa didn't have the limp. From the coveralls to the impish grin and short-fuse temper, Amos McCoy and my grandfather were the mirror image of each other; although the resemblance was not in their faces, their character and values were identical. Watching this hardworking farmer who sometimes became a bit unappreciative of modern inventions and "newfangled" ideas, I often wondered whether my grandfather recognized the similarities himself and whether that is why he liked the show so much. I used to love hearing Gramps chuckle and laugh at the antics of the character that I thought was so much the embodiment of him. He was, in fact, the real McCoy!

In his usual work overalls with Olive
Bennett, looking like the Real McCoy!

Sometimes, Gramps would make popcorn the old-fashioned way on top of the wood stove. He would often bring some to us kids next door, but occasionally, I would catch him on a night when he had made some with real butter and salted to yummy taste. Another treat that he would often have on his person was Black Jack chewing gum. I adored the licorice taste, and even though I occasionally find it and buy some now, it never tastes quite the same as when Grampa would give me a stick from his pocket stash.

Winter meant the hay was in the loft and the woodshed was full, so the biggest chore of the season was shoveling snow! When a real Nor'easter blew in from the coast, it could drop snow measured in feet, not just inches, over hours. It was times like this that Grampa would melt candle wax on the snow shovel and ready himself for the big task ahead. It was usually him and me battling the storm and my father too if it was nighttime and he was home from work. My father was on-call because he drove an ambulance part-time for the town as well as working his regular job. It was imperative that no matter how much snow fell, my father had to get to work, and we had to go to school if there was school the next day. That meant, in our family, that you shoveled as long as the snow was coming down, and that might mean nearly all night. Just as we cleared the driveway, the plow would come down the street and pile up a big barrier at the end of the drive, and so we kept going outside and clearing the snow.

Grampa would shovel a path out back to the burn barrel where he would burn the trash, not allowed these days in our environmentally conscious world. He shoveled the walks on the front side of the house, in case an ambulance needed access, the drive, a path to the barn to do the milking (when we had the cow), and an area under the clothesline because dryers did not exist in my family, although they may have been in the stores. We shoveled the walk in the back to the woodshed, and after the storm was over the next day, he would often shovel a path out onto the lawn side so that the water from the melting snow had a place to run off to instead of into the cellar. We shoveled together, and we shoveled in shifts, constantly preventing the buildup of snow more than a few inches, and even with those best efforts, we were shoveling through a foot or more when it fell like a blizzard.

Now, I will argue that there were good reasons for being so diligent. As a result, we were often the only family on the street the next morning with a cleared driveway, able to get the cars out, and my father could get to work. If we were fortunate enough to have the next day off from school, the bulk of the shoveling done, I rested or sledded or built snow forts, depending on how much snow was on the ground. What is the lesson here? My grandfather and the rest of my family believed in hard work and preparation and did not succumb to chance or bad fate. One cannot control the weather, but the fortitude and willpower that I learned from these times were a lesson for life. I must admit that by the awful winter of 1968–69, I was fed up with shoveling, and I left for the air force in February. I told the recruiter, "Get me out of here—I am tired of shoveling snow!"

CHAPTER 18
THANKSGIVING AND CHRISTMAS

We always celebrated Thanksgiving dinner at my grandmother's side of the house, and we really had two Christmas mornings, one in each side of the duplex where we lived. Except for the Thanksgiving that my brother and I had chicken pox and were quarantined to our rooms, Thanksgiving dinner was a crowded ordeal at my grandmother's table. In addition to the five of us, my grandparents, Aunt Virginia, and Uncle Ed, we were also joined by Aunt Edith and Uncle Wilmer—eleven people in a small kitchen with a twenty-two-pound turkey and all the fixings. It was in many ways a Norman Rockwell moment. Some today argue that this idea of a nuclear-family holiday was a myth and did not ever exist. I am here to say that I know the reality existed for me and many families like us. In the hectic, pessimistic atmosphere and sensory overload of today, with so many distractions, there has been a loss of these traditional family scenes, and a loss in the accompanying values of home resulted too. The big tradition in our day was watching the Macy's Parade on the television, which was over by eleven o'clock or noon at the latest, and by two o'clock, we were full into the turkey and pumpkin pie. But we were together all day.

Thanksgiving table with everyone around.

Christmas was delegated to my mother's side of the duplex, in order to distribute the holiday workload. The same faces and characters were present, except that some years we also were visited by my maternal grandfather, later in the afternoon. My grandfather would toast with wine, and sometimes, as I said before, he and my uncle would have a bit too much, which only brought out the mischievous playfulness that my grampa enjoyed. Sometimes this irritated my mother and father to no end, and my mother hated the drinking (even though in her younger days I had seen her drink a cocktail such as a Rob Roy, or a screwdriver, but never more than one). She was very judgmental and sometimes, I thought, a bit "holier than thou," which is not a compliment to her Catholic upbringing but explains a lot. My father, likewise, never drank much, and the only time I ever saw him totally wasted was on my tenth birthday, when Uncle Wilmer seemed to have temporarily abducted him for some manly reason. I think what set things off was the envy my father had about the close bonding I seemed to enjoy with my grandparents. There was no doubt that I was their "favorite," and with their having only three grandchildren, and with my being the oldest, this may have been natural even if not right.

Grampa and Uncle Ed making merry.
That is Aunt Edith in the back.

Gramps's biggest joke every Christmas was to give my mother a ladies undergarment, just to see the always-embarrassed look on her face when she opened the present. She must have come to expect it after a time because she would begin to say, when my grandfather handed her the gift, "Oh, I bet I know what this is." He liked teasing her in that way, and I think he liked her more than he would admit or let on. He almost always called her by her first name, Barbara, and that had significance.

The tension would sometimes rise to an uncomfortable level during the holidays, so those days sometimes ended on a bad note. You knew when my grandfather was really angry because he could shout and cuss and huff and puff, with eyes flaring, in a way you would not forget. But he cooled down almost as quickly, and I can't say he ever carried a grudge, though he may have in the recesses of his mind. My father not only would blow up in a similar fashion but also would seethe for days, and you could tell anger was below the surface. Whether the conversation was serious or not, my grandfather had a habit of calling people "Bub." Now, initially, this might seem derogatory, and the name certainly could be used in such a manner, but most of the time, he said it as term of endearment. When he was trying to make a point, he would often end his sentence with "Bub," such as "I'll tell you what, Bub!" He would also use the nickname in everyday conversation—for example, "Hey, Bub, you awake yet?" In any instance, it was easy for it to sound condescending, and I think it irritated my father immensely. He applied the term only to men; his term for women when he wanted to emphasize his position was "Missy." I do not think he was being mean on purpose, though today it would hardly seem polite or politically correct. It was his way, I think, of establishing himself as the family patriarch, and I was never offended when he called me "Bub." He also would refer to me or my father as "Boy." Again, I did not take offense because I was so much younger than he, but I feel my father resented it. I cannot recall my grandfather calling my father by his name, Edwin, except rare instances to his face, and any time he referred to my father with me, he did so in the third person: "your father."

Gramps seemed to never let anything bother him for very long. He knew how to have a good time, and he could get angry, but he also possessed an inner peace that I have seen in few people. He never had much in the way of wealth his whole life and had to work hard for everything, but even in the most dire situations, when life seemed to mount against him, he never would worry about tomorrow or when his next meal was coming or what you might have thought of him.

Grampa with his celebratory wine. Can you see the twinkle in his eye?

CHAPTER 19
CHURCHGOING MAN

Grampa was not what you would refer to as a religious man, but he was a faithful member of the Methodist Church. He held appropriate levels of responsibility over the years and attended more or less on a regular basis. The story is that my father used to frequent a Baptist church in the town where we lived, which was no longer viable by the time I came along, and my mother had been raised a Catholic, so the differences of faith were tremendous. In the 1940s and '50s, this was a real mixed marriage. That was one of the reasons for the existing animosity between my mother and my father's family. How we came to be Methodists, I'm not quite clear, but it was some sort of consensus.

We were made to attend Sunday school regardless, and I made my confirmation at twelve dutifully. My mother insisted that we were to become educated in the church, and when we were old enough to decide for ourselves, we could choose what faith we followed accordingly. My pin for years of perfect Sunday school attendance was a testimony to my mother's nonnegotiable rule. Following Sunday school was church, and my grandparents would be there as convenience would allow. If the garden was not a pressing issue, they would be in the pew with us, and we would all sit in the proper hierarchical order, from Grampa at the end all the way down. I remember well the brown pinstripe suit he wore for years, circa 1930s, until he obtained a blue pinstripe of the same style. He was most likely buried in one of them.

Grampa would sing along with the hymns but had a voice like a bucket of rocks. My grandmother had a high, wavering falsetto singing voice, so the cacophony of sounds coming from our pew must have been something to the ears of the preacher. I never discussed God or religion with Grampa. It was enough, I guess, that he lived the values of a Christian soul without philosophizing about it.

The scriptures tell us life is long, and we should rejoice in it before the dark of death overcomes us. I was taught that God holds us to account and that a futile and empty life is meaningless before judgment. I believe Grampa thought the same, although he did not preach about it. Instead, he demonstrated by the way he lived his life that there is little to be gained by worrying about the end of days and that life is worth living only in the here and now.

CHAPTER 20
ENJOY LIFE WITH THE ONE YOU LOVE

Grampa was always surprising me in ways he never knew. I played the guitar some when I was in my teens, or I attempted to, and I decided it would be neat to learn the harmonica as well, so I bought one. When Gramps saw my pitiful attempt at playing it, he said, "Let me see that," and I'm certain my mouth dropped in awe. He played a tune on the thing like it was no feat at all, and although I had never seen him play before, I was so impressed with this revelation I didn't know what to say. He was like that.

On another day when he was well into his sixties, he took my bike and was riding it up and down our street. This isn't perhaps such a great feat, but when you see your not-quite-agile grampa doing something you have never seen before, it is quite surprising. He was, after all, a youngster at heart. We often forget that older people have skills and are capable of doing so much more than we give them credit for.

Grampa and my bike.

He was always generous to a fault, which disturbed me at times. I felt people took advantage of him. He was frugal but never seemed to save a dime. Most of the property he and my grandmother owned—mostly pasture and hay fields and pine forest—had come into the family from my grandmother's inheritance. But as was the custom or tradition, they owned it jointly, and certainly my grandfather's years of sweat equity purchased his portion fair and square. Years previously, they had deeded the town acreage in the middle of one of our fields for a new water tank to supply the town with water. Ironically, our house was one of the few on its own well, so we did not have the advantage of the commercial water supply until many years later. They owned the highest point of land around, so the tower was built there, on our land. Then the town needed a new septic field for the town's sewage system.

Because we owned the land adjacent, my grandparents again deeded to the town the available land. I am not aware of any compensation for these land grants. My parents just said, "They gave the land to the town."

The grade school I attended for my first four years of school was adjacent to our cow pasture. It closed when the town built a new elementary school that combined the grade schools from three areas. After it was vacant, the American Legion decided it would be a good idea to convert the old school into the location for their new post, and guess what— my grandfather gave away a good-size chunk of our adjacent land to that organization as well. My grandparents sold off some other land in sections not connected to the main portion deeded to our house. In each instance, though the details are fuzzy, they never received just compensation for the value of the lands. One deal that was especially frustrating involved land along the lake where I used to swim and fish as a boy. It was but a strip along the shoreline, but it was purchased by adjacent landowners for a song. Although I felt my grandparents' generosity was never appreciated by others, it was their property and their legacy.

My grandfather also always gave generously to the "Home for Little Wanderers," an orphanage near Boston, as I recall. I have no doubt that some connection from his past was the reason for this, though I didn't realize it at the time.

He bought my grandmother a beautiful red ruby ring when they were quite elderly. I don't know if it was maybe to make up for something from long ago, but the expense of the gift and the generosity surprised even me. He was always a giving person, whether he was providing vegetables from the garden, a soda or hamburger for me, land, or expensive displays of affection for my grandmother. He would give you what he had if you needed it.

Grampa and Gramma on their fiftieth anniversary in 1968.

Chapter 21
The Cauliflower

Grampa was proud to be a farmer his entire life. He raised record-breaking vegetables. Sometimes he would receive notoriety for his more than two-pound potatoes or his large deliciously sweet strawberries. Mostly he was known locally for his quality produce and fair dealings. He attended the Big Eastern States Exposition every year as an annual ritual, as well as local county fairs, to which, of course, I went along if possible. He loved farms and farming—the animals, the dirt, the production of farm goods, anything and everything about farming. Although he would not admit it, he also loved flowers, and I once assisted him in planting a rhododendron bush in our front yard that thrives today as well as many of his rose bushes. I'm sure if there is a heaven for him, it is a working farm.

One day we got on to a conversation about funerals. Someone had died, and I guess we were discussing flowers for the funeral when he said a most curious thing. He said,

"When I die, don't waste your money on cut flowers that will just die and go to waste. Buy me a cauliflower. Then take it home and eat it." I don't know why, but that stayed with me, representative of his frugalness and practicality while proclaiming a sort of false machismo that I saw clearly through.

By the late 1970s, Grampa was well into his eighties and I saw him only on my infrequent visits home. Each time, I could see the gradual deterioration as his tiring body aged. I remember quite vividly the image of him sitting on a bench at the airport, waiting for my plane. Within a couple minutes of sitting still, he usually fell asleep and seemed to be tired most of the time as all the years of labor began to overtake him. It was during these years that he required a back operation. He suffered from degenerative disc disease and spinal arthritis, the same hereditary affliction that affects me today. At the hospital it was said that he was one of the oldest recipients of such an operation at that time. The postoperative prognosis was that he would be bedridden for weeks and months, for a slow recovery, given his age. But within three days, Grampa refused to use the crutches to get out of bed and walk, and by the end of the week, he was going up and down the stairs. The hospital staff was shocked and amazed by his recovery and positive attitude. They obviously did not know my grandfather or his intestinal fortitude and belief that there was no such word as "can't."

Grampa died January 21, 1985. I was in the air force at the time, stationed in Arizona. The news struck me very hard, and for reasons enough, I knew I would not be able to get home for the funeral in time. I don't think I wanted to go—because I knew the pain and sorrow of loss would be more than I could humanly bear. I was a grown man, a military officer, but I often broke down and wept bitterly for days. I still do when I think about it. I called the florist whom we had used for years for such occasions to order an arrangement for his funeral. I recall telling the florist that I had a rather odd request and wondered if it would be a problem. "In the wreath," I told her, "I want you to place a cauliflower among the arrangement." She told me that she understood and that it was not such an odd request at all. She said it with sincerity, and I believed her. Later, as I spoke with my family on the phone, they told me that everyone who had attended the wake and funeral had remarked about how appropriate the cauliflower seemed, given that he loved to garden so much. For a long time afterward, I never told anyone of our private conversation or the real reason I ordered the cauliflower.

I finally made it back to Massachusetts about a month later, near his birth date of February 26. It had been a typical New England winter, cold for weeks, and the day I visited the gravesite, it was bitterly cold as well. As I approached the family plot, it wasn't hard to pick out the new grave with its pile of faded, wilted flowers that a month before had been in full bloom and glory. There, contrasted against the dead, dull flowers, sat the cauliflower, as fresh-looking as one you might see in the market today, perfect in color, well preserved in the cold winter air. The tears welled up as I stood there, knowing he had waited for me to say my final good-bye.

In August 1985, I was once again home on leave, about to be transferred overseas. Having sold my car, I borrowed my grandmother's 1968 Dodge Coronet to spend a day at the beach with an old friend and buddy I had not seen in years. That evening while driving home, I passed the road that led to the cemetery where Grampa was buried. The road on which I was traveling was adjacent to the hill where the cemetery was hidden by the trees. My thoughts were of my grandfather and how close we were both physically and spiritually at that moment. I could feel his essence with me in the car. Suddenly, a bright pair of headlights filled the windshield as a car rounded the curve up ahead. In that instant, I knew the car coming toward me was not going to negotiate the turn successfully as my mind raced to calculate its speed, vector, and point of impact. Temporarily blinded by the headlights, I hit the brake and turned the car toward the ditch. It was too late, and through either instinct or the force of the crash, I found myself across the front seat. The car that crashed into me was a late 1960s model Pontiac Bonneville, a behemoth of a car, and it caught me nearly head-on.

In the moments after the crash, I could not open my driver's side door. Still dazed and trying to recover my senses and eyeglasses, I was able to crawl out the passenger side door. Fortunately, I appeared to have only some minor bumps and bruises. When I surveyed the wreckage the next day, I saw that the engine was pushed well up under the dashboard and that the driver's side door was folded in and pushed behind the steering wheel where I sat. Maybe it was the size of the old Dodge, but there was no way I should have survived the crash, let alone escaped with only minor bruises. The car was emphatically totaled. I believe my grandfather was riding as my guardian angel that night. There is no way anyone can convince me otherwise.

CHAPTER 22
THE FINAL TRIBUTE

When my grandmother followed my grandfather to their final reward in December 1988, I did not attend her funeral either because I was stationed overseas. When I did make it home once again, I went to a local tree farm and selected an evergreen to place at the gravesite of my beloved grandparents. It was because I knew I would not be in New England every year to place flowers on their graves every Memorial Day, as was our family tradition. The evergreen would be a constant, growing, living tribute to people who had so loved me and influenced my life. The tree thrived and grew taller each year, and my parents would keep me apprized of its progress every time they visited the cemetery. When I once again had the chance to visit the site, I noticed a most wonderful and amazing feature to this tree. When I had purchased it, it was the size of a shrub and looked no different from any other tree of its kind. Now, however, it had grown tall and straight, but at the very top, it had developed two tops, two distinct peaks, almost as if it were two trees joined together as one! To me the twin peaks were a final tribute to two people I loved dearly and who influenced my life so much. I had never seen such a thing in my life, the new growth at the top pointing straight up to the sky. It was a final tribute from the universe to a common man, a farmer who loved to watch new life grow. Whatever your personal thoughts of God are, I think he must be a farmer too.

Grampa and Gramma circa 1980.

AFTERWORD

What does it mean for a man to live an entire life and then leave this earthly existence with no mark or indication of his existence? I know this theme has been pursued by other authors, such as Rick Warren in *The Purpose Driven Life,* and certainly is explored in the Bible (Ecclesiastes 12:1–8). What is the purpose of a man's life? Every life has purpose, and the challenge is to discover that purpose at some point in each life. This book is a memoir and a record of a common man who was neither famous nor wealthy. He, like many others have and will, lived decades on this earth and simply passed on, unnoticed by most of the world. For that reason, my grandfather's life is similar to those of many others who seem to pass through this physical realm without notice. Still, I want to recognize not only his life but also the lives of so many other common men and women who live and die in obscurity, save for the few lives they touched while here on Earth.

No life is that small or insignificant that it does not leave its mark. We need to remind ourselves of this when the brunt force of life bears down on us. Chester Warren Roaf was born out of a broken home and never knew his birth father, and it is doubtful, from all indications, that he even knew his mother. Abandoned young, and having to make his way through the world, he needed character and strong will to survive. We often hear from psychologists how important nurturing is to a person's development. Yet without the nurturing environment of a traditional family, my grandfather still developed strong character traits that served him during his life and inspired me and others as well. A whole town came to know his generosity. Neighbors and friends knew him as a hardworking, humble, and honest man. He possessed a sense of humor and a zest for life without the yoke of depression that hangs over so many people.

Though he was detached from his siblings at a young age, his never-say-die attitude led him to find and reestablish relationships with three of his long-lost family members. In spite of not having a close-knit family environment in early life, he grew to love family as his own family respected him as a patriarch. My grandfather's riches did not come from material things but from within his own soul.

As I stated at the beginning, he was a teacher, mentor, friend, companion, philosopher, and so much more to me personally, and somehow, his legacy and others like his must never be forgotten. The principles and values my grandfather possessed in his life are still important character traits: honesty, integrity, ingenuity, humor, humility, and self-driven motivation are keys to anyone's success. It is my hope, therefore, that this book has given you a smile and perhaps a tear or two, but also and most importantly, a newfound hope that all is not lost and the knowledge that however small a contribution, each of our lives has meaning. I conclude with this passage from Ecclesiastes 9:14–16:

> There was a little city with few men in it, and a great king came against it and besieged it, building great siege-works against it. But there was found in it a poor wise man, and he by his wisdom, delivered the city. Yet no one remembered that poor man. But I say that wisdom is better than might, though the poor man's wisdom is despised and his words are not heeded.